I0820954

HORSE BREEDS

AMERICAN QUARTER HORSE

BY WHITNEY SANDERSON

Kids Core

An Imprint of Abdo Publishing
abdobooks.com

abdobooks.com

Published by Abdo Publishing, a division of ABDO, PO Box 398166, Minneapolis, Minnesota 55439. Copyright © 2026 by Abdo Consulting Group, Inc. International copyrights reserved in all countries. No part of this book may be reproduced in any form without written permission from the publisher. Kids Core™ is a trademark and logo of Abdo Publishing.

Printed in the United States of America, North Mankato, Minnesota.
052025
092025

THIS BOOK CONTAINS
RECYCLED MATERIALS

Cover Photo: Jaco Wiid/Shutterstock Images
Interior Photos: Shutterstock Images, 4–5, 10, 20–21, 22, 25 (bottom right); Liz Neb/Shutterstock Images, 7; Arco/A. Schmelzer/imageBROKER.com GmbH & Co. KG/Alamy, 8, 28–29; Alfredo de Luna/VW Pics/Universal Images Group/Getty Images, 9; Dagmara Ksandrova/Shutterstock Images, 12–13; Detroit Photographic Co./Library of Congress, 15; Underwood Archives/Archive Photos/Getty Images, 17; Kit Leong/Shutterstock Images, 18; Jose Luis Raota/Moment/Getty Images, 24; Wayne Gooden/Alamy, 25 (top left); Carol Walker/Nature Picture Library/Alamy, 25 (top right); Warren Price Photography/Shutterstock Images, 25 (bottom left); wanderluster/E+/Getty Images, 26

Editor: Marie Pearson
Series Designer: Ryan Gale

Library of Congress Control Number: 2024949190

Publisher's Cataloging-in-Publication Data

Names: Sanderson, Whitney, author.
Title: American quarter horse / by Whitney Sanderson
Description: Minneapolis, Minnesota: Abdo Publishing, 2026 | Series: Horse breeds | Includes online resources and index.
Identifiers: ISBN 9781098297473 (lib. bdg.) | ISBN 9798384919995 (ebook)
Subjects: LCSH: Quarter horse--Juvenile literature. | Horses--Juvenile literature. | Horse breeds--Juvenile literature. | Zoology--Juvenile literature.
Classification: DDC 636.13--dc23

CONTENTS

Ranchers often use horses to cover large areas of rough ground.

CHAPTER 1

COW SENSE

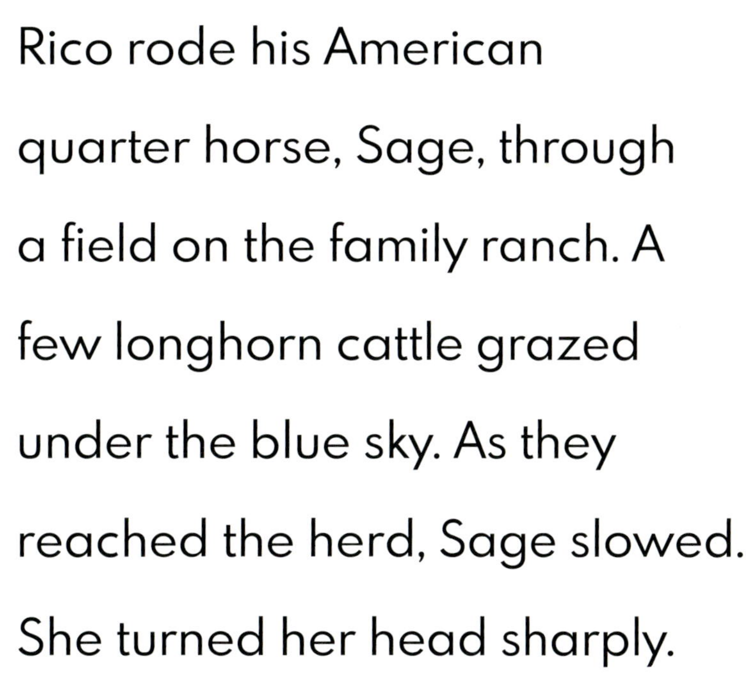

Rico rode his American quarter horse, Sage, through a field on the family ranch. A few longhorn cattle grazed under the blue sky. As they reached the herd, Sage slowed. She turned her head sharply.

Her sensitive ears had picked up a sound that Rico couldn't hear.

Sage wanted to turn left. Rico let her. The clever **bay** mare could always tell when something was wrong in the herd.

Sage brought them to a dry streambed with steep sides. Now Rico heard a low *moo*. A mother cow stood at the edge of the bank. She shook her head and pawed the ground. Her calf had slipped into the rocky ravine.

Rico slid down from Sage's back. He tied a rope to Sage's saddle horn. "Whoa, Sage," he said. Sage stood still while Rico climbed down into the ravine with the rope.

Rico looped the rope around the calf's body. He made sure it was snug but not too tight.

Ranchers can use horses to move cattle from one field to another.

"Pull, Sage!" Rico called. He made a clicking sound with his tongue. Sage stepped back. The rope tightened. The calf began to rise out of the ravine. Rico stayed nearby to help guide it.

It takes a lot of training to get a reliable ranch horse.

At last, the calf was safely on solid ground. Rico untied the rope and set the calf free. It trotted to its mother. She nuzzled her baby. The hungry calf began to nurse.

Some quarter horses are trustworthy for children to ride.

Rico ruffled Sage's black mane. "What do you say? Is it time for our dinner too?" Sage had definitely earned her hay and oats. Running a cattle ranch was hard work. But Rico could count on his trusty quarter horse to get the job done.

The quarter horse is the state horse of Oklahoma and Texas.

America's Horse

The American quarter horse is a breed best known for its speed and **agility**. Many quarter horses have cow sense, or a natural ability to work with cattle.

Built for Speed

A quarter horse **stallion** named First Moonflash made history. He earned the world record for fastest time in a quarter-mile (0.4-km) race. In 2009, he ran that distance in 20.27 seconds!

The breed is named for its sprinting ability. Quarter horses are the fastest breed in the world for up to a quarter of a mile (0.4 km). They can reach speeds of 55 miles per hour (89 km/h)! That is as fast as a car driving on the highway. More than 6 million quarter horses are **registered** today. That makes them the most popular breed in the United States!

Further Evidence

Read the article below. Does it give any new evidence to support Chapter One?

Explore 18 Breeds of Horses

abdocorelibrary.com/american-quarter-horse

The quarter horse was one of the first North American horse breeds.

CHAPTER 2

HISTORY OF THE QUARTER HORSE

In the 1600s, English settlers brought horses to North America. They were mostly plow horses used to work in the fields. The settlers sometimes raced their horses. They often held races on their towns' main streets.

Main streets usually ran about a quarter mile (0.4 km). The settlers' horses were bred for heavy work. Most of them weren't very fast.

The Chickasaw people of the southeastern United States had fast horses. Chickasaw horses were descendants of a breed called the Spanish Barb. Settlers from Spain brought these horses in the 1500s. American settlers traded for some of the Chickasaw horses. They bred them with their farm horses. The result was a new breed with the speed of Chickasaw horses and the strength of English horses.

A **stallion** named Janus was one horse who helped create the quarter horse. He was a prize-winning racehorse in England. His owners brought him to the United States in the 1750s.

At first, people called the horses bred from Chickasaw and settler horses the "Celebrated American quarter running horse." Later this was shortened to quarter horse.

Janus was the son of the Godolphin Arabian, who helped create the Thoroughbred breed. Janus had many foals with Chickasaw mares, which are female horses.

Western Stars

From the 1840s to 1860s, settlers on the East Coast began to move west. The western plains had a lot of open land that was good for raising cattle. Quarter horses turned out to be great ranch horses. They helped ranchers move cattle from place to place.

Steel Dust

Steel Dust was a horse used to develop the quarter horse. He was born in Kentucky in 1843 and then moved to Texas with his owners. He won race after race against the fastest horses of his day. He became so famous that his sons and daughters were called "Steel Dusts."

Some performers did stunts on quarter horses for audiences in the 1930s.

As towns formed in the West, people held rodeos for entertainment. These rowdy contests showed off horses' skills with cattle. They tested the horses' speed and agility.

The AQHA runs the American Quarter Horse Hall of Fame and Museum in Amarillo, Texas.

The American Quarter Horse Association (AQHA) started in 1940. It keeps a registry of all quarter horses that are born. The AQHA also decides the breed standard for what a quarter horse should look like.

The government of Texas made the quarter horse the official state horse in 2009. It said:

> The American quarter horse first caught the attention of many during the cattle drives of the late 1800s; strong, smart, fast, and tough, the animal was perfectly suited to the task of carrying cowboys.

Source: "Texas State Horse—American Quarter Horse." *Washington on the Brazos*, n.d., wheretexasbecametexas.org. Accessed 2 Dec. 2024.

What's the Big Idea?

Read the quote carefully. What is the main idea? How is it supported by details? Name two or three details that support the main idea.

Muscular hindquarters give quarter horses a lot of speed in short bursts.

LIVING WITH THE QUARTER HORSE

Quarter horses are built for powerful sprints and quick turns. They have a muscular build, a broad chest, and powerful hindquarters. Their heads are small and straight when seen from the side.

Cremello horses often have blue eyes.

The most common color for quarter horses is sorrel, a bright reddish brown. Other colors are bay, gray, black, **roan**, **buckskin**, and **palomino**. A special gene gives some quarter horses rare colors called cremello and perlino.

Cremello is a shiny cream color. Perlino is cream colored with a reddish mane.

A Diverse Breed

Quarter horses stand between 14.2 and 17 hands high. A hand is 4 inches (10 cm). Quarter horses weigh 1,000 to 1,500 pounds (450–680 kg).

Healing with Horses

Equine-assisted therapy is a type of riding meant to improve the physical and mental health of riders with disabilities. In 2023, a quarter horse named Cheerioak won a $10,000 award from the AQHA for his work with many riders. Some of his riders included former members of the armed forces in the Wounded Warrior Project.

People breed quarter horses for different jobs.

There are several types of quarter horses. The stock type is the shortest. It is used for ranch work and Western events such as barrel racing. The halter type is muscular with a delicate head. The racing type has longer legs. The hunter type is tall and graceful so it can clear jumps.

Quarter horses are good at many kinds of riding sports. They often win prizes in Western events. These events are based on ranch work. Quarter horses still work on ranches today.

Western Events

Barrel Racing

The horse and rider gallop around three barrels in a cloverleaf pattern.

Team Penning

Three horses and riders work together to separate specific cows from a herd and put them in a pen.

Calf Roping

A mounted rider chases and ropes a calf. The rider ties three of the calf's legs with a piece of rope.

Reining

The rider shows off the horse's skill in moves such as spins, circles, and fast stops.

These are just a few of the Western riding events that quarter horses compete in.

Quarter horses can make fun companions.

Quarter horses also do well in English events such as jumping, **dressage**, and pulling carts. Their friendly, willing nature makes them popular horses for lesson barns. From roping a cow on a ranch to taking a young rider on their first trail ride, a quarter horse can do it all!

Explore Online

Watch this video about the quarter horse. How does the information in it compare with what is written in this chapter? Is any of it the same? Is any of it different?

Why the Quarter Horse Is Built for Speed

abdocorelibrary.com/american-quarter-horse

BREED TRAITS

Muscular body
Small head
Deep chest
Strong legs

Glossary

agility
the ability to start, turn, and stop quickly

bay
brown with a black mane and tail

buckskin
a tan or gold coat color with a black mane and tail

dressage
a sport in which a horse and rider perform graceful patterns with very small cues from the rider

palomino
a gold coat color with a white mane and tail

registered
listed as a member of an organization

roan
a color with white and dark hairs mixed together

stallion
a male horse who can have offspring

Online Resources

To learn more about American quarter horses and other horses, visit our free resource websites below.

Visit **abdocorelibrary.com** or scan this QR code for free Common Core resources for teachers and students, including vetted activities, multimedia, and booklinks, for deeper subject comprehension.

Visit **abdobooklinks.com** or scan this QR code for free additional online weblinks for further learning. These links are routinely monitored and updated to provide the most current information available.

Learn More

Mazzarella, Kerri. *American Quarter Horse.* Crabtree, 2024.

Pearson, Marie. *Horse Behavior.* Abdo, 2024.

Ventura, Marne. *Horses.* Abdo, 2023.

Index

About the Author

Whitney Sanderson grew up riding horses as a member of a 4-H club and competing in local horse shows. She is the author of numerous children's books.